Contents

Acknowledgements
The publishers would like to thank
Wilsons for their photographic
contribution to this book.

Thanks to Alexandra Palace ice rink and
Queens ice skating club.
Photograph on page 29 (right) courtesy
of Kimberley Haggis. Photographs on the
inside front cover, pages 26 and 27, and
the inside back cover courtesy of Allsport
UK Ltd. Photographs on pages 1, 37, 40,
42 and 43 courtesy of Sporting Pictures
(UK) Ltd.
All other photographs by Denise Taylor.
Illustrations by Michael Bartlett.

Note   Throughout the book skaters are
referred to individually as 'he'. This
should, of course, be taken to mean 'he
or she' where appropriate.

National Ice Skating Association
of Great Britain
15–17 Gee Street
London
EC1V 3RE

tel 071 253 3824/0910

Introduction

Ice skating is one of the most exciting
yet relaxing sports in which anyone can
participate. How exciting it is depends
upon you, and on how energetic and
adventurous you are. If you want to
tear around, jumping and spinning,
then the possibilities exist; if, on the
other hand, you simply want to take
gentle exercise, then you can do that
too. Ice skating is therefore an ideal
sport for all types and all ages.

Because of the public interest following the international success of various
British skaters, there are now dozens of
rinks spread over the UK, with the result
that most people have one within
reasonably easy reach. To find out
where your local ice rink is, contact the
national skating organisation in your
country. (In the UK this is the National
Ice Skating Association, the address of
which is on this page.)

As a recreational pastime skating is
inexpensive, usually costing less than a
trip to the movies or a cheap meal out.
In general, rinks have reasonable
snack-bars (and licensed bars) and
superb equipment shops; most also
have great sound systems playing suitably inspirational music, together with
either television-type lighting for the
serious practice sessions or flashing
effects or video screens for the disco session skaters.

For those who wish to improve their
skating techniques, individual lessons
and/or group tuition are available in a
friendly social atmosphere. If you take
part in the various group classes you
can meet skaters of all ages and from all
backgrounds. You will have great fun,
at the same time helping each other
through the basic moves under the
supervision of a professional coach.
These 'How To Skate' programmes
generally consist of mother-and-child
classes, children's classes and adult
classes.   Mother-and-child   classes
encourage mothers to learn to skate
along with their under-fives. Children's
classes are for those between the
approximate ages of five and 15; while

adult classes are for anyone older than 15 and are structured around a skating award scheme, such as that organised by the National Ice Skating Association of Great Britain. Classes provide the best introduction to ice skating, and you should ask at your local ice rink for the relevant information.

As you progress, you will also be able to take private lessons (generally 15 minutes in length) with a professional coach. (The financial outlay involved in such lessons will soon bring the dividends of much faster progress.) For those young enough there is always the possibility of becoming a champion; while those who are a little older can enjoy the dance intervals and enter club competitions.

Perhaps the most beneficial aspect of the sport is the promotion of health and general well-being. It also provides the opportunity to bump (perhaps literally!) into some really interesting people and progress together – whether you are two years old or 72.

Equipment

As is the case with most sports, the use of correct specific equipment is very important. You will need strong boots with well-made blades, and you should wear comfortable, loose-fitting clothes.

Footwear

Boots

A skating boot is usually made of several layers of thick leather or plastic, reinforced in various strategic places (particularly the heel and instep) to hold the wearer's ankle correctly during the wide range of skating moves. The boot comes some way up the ankle and is fastened with laces running through eyelets and over hooks.

Boot ▶

3

Blades

The blade is made of metal coated in chrome, and has two edges that are formed by cutting a concave/hollow into the underside. These are known as the *outside* and *inside edges* (corresponding to the outside and inside of the foot). At the front end there are a series of sharp points, called *toe picks*, which are generally used for jumping (**not for stopping**). The blade is attached to the sole and heel of the skating boot by way of screws.

Clothing for your first few sessions

All new skaters should make sure that they are sensibly and comfortably clad. Be sure to wear loose and preferably stretchy clothing – track suits or jogging trousers and sweatshirts are ideal. (Tight jeans are about as unsuitable as you can get!) Avoid long jackets, hats, scarves and anything else that might either restrict your movement or drop on to the ice and be a hazard to you or any other skater. You should wear gloves to protect your hands. Little

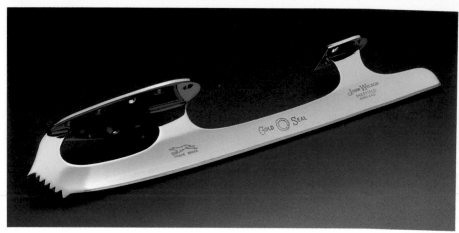

▲ *Free skating blade*

▲ *Dance blade*

4

children under the age of five must wear either an ice hockey helmet or a thick woollen hat for protection.

It's a good idea to wear something with a pocket, so that you have somewhere to put your snack money, your locker key and a copy of this book.

Never wear personal stereos on the ice – I have seen people accidently drop and break them, and the bits of plastic cause hazardous conditions for their fellow skaters.

Advanced skaters usually wear close-fitting outfits made of stretchy material such as lycra, so their movements are not restricted at any time. These outfits are designed to show off the bodylines of the wearers as effectively as possible. It must be said that the spectacular and often highly original costumes worn by top skaters for competition should be avoided by newcomers. Such outfits are not designed to withstand the rigours of practice sessions and would cause a certain amount of mirth amongst fellow skaters.

Girls/women

Girls and women should wear skating dresses. For practice it's advisable to buy a dark colour: black is ideal. Don't buy a skating dress until you have at least mastered the basics (reasonable forward and backward skating and three turns). For practice many girls wear thick, dark tights with their dresses.

Boys/men

Boys and men should wear two-way stretch trousers (trousers that can stretch vertically). These should be fitted with elastic straps, so that they can be fastened underneath the skater's boots to ensure a good leg line, essential for all competitors.

You will probably have to find somebody to make these trousers for you as few suppliers, apart perhaps from ballroom dance outfitters, stock them. Often, however, someone specialises in making skating clothes, so it is worth enquiring.

Your skate-hire boots

When you collect your skating boots from the skate hire, you should check them carefully using the following guidelines. First, you should assess the general condition of the boots. The laces must be in reasonable condition, not frayed, and all the eyelets must be in place. Second, you should check the blades and especially the state of their edges. This can be done by scraping your finger nail across one edge then the other. If a little of the nail surface comes away, you have an edge; if not, the blades need to be sharpened. If this is the case, you should ask for another pair.

Fasten the boots by carefully drawing the laces together, then catch them against the eyelets and tie them securely at the top. To check they are fastened correctly, stand with your feet together then try to bend your knees. If the boots resist a great deal and you are unable to bend your knees, you should loosen them slightly. If the boots are wobbly, then refasten, making them a little tighter.

If you are unhappy with the boots in any way, take them back and ask for another pair.

Buying your boots and skates

Your first pair of boots and skates will most probably be what is known as a 'set'. This amounts to a pair of skating

▲ *Fastening your boots*

boots with blades already attached. As you progress you will move on to buy specific makes of boots and blades which are sold separately.

In my experience most of the good ice skating equipment is imported from continental Europe – Austria in particular – or the United States, so if you happen to visit either of these countries it might be worthwhile buying your boots and blades at the same time.

Custom-made boots

Many of the top skaters, as well as those people who want a boot specifically made to fit their feet, use custom-made boots. (Schindelar's ice skating boots of Austria are well known for this purpose.) The skater sends an outline of his feet, together with various measurements and the strength required (dance strength through to very rigid), and the boots are then made to these precise specifications.

How your blades should be fitted

Most ice rinks and equipment suppliers will ensure that your blades are correctly fitted to your boots. It must be said that personal preference is an important factor in how this is done and where the blades are positioned. The fact that a blade is perfectly positioned dead-centre of the skate is no guarantee that it is correctly placed for you. Personally, I have my left blade set slightly to the outside; others may prefer different settings.

In order to check that the blade positioning is right for you, you can try out the following test. (*Note* This test assumes you can skate the Stage 3 forward skating described on page 10.) Hold your arms firmly out to the side, take a couple of pushes to gather speed, then stand on the left foot, keeping both edges of the right skate in contact with the ice and travelling in a straight line. If you are able to do this without the skate pulling to the left or right, then it is correctly fitted for you. If the left blade pulls to the left, it may need to be moved slightly in the other direction (inwards). If the blade pulls to the right, it may need to be moved slightly to the left (outwards). Your ice rink should be able to advise and make the adjustment for you.

Protective clothing

Apart from gloves and helmets (for small children) there are a variety of knee, elbow and bottom pads available from the better skating equipment suppliers.

Equipment care

Your boots and skates are costly, precision-made items and as such should be treated with a good deal of care. Before each skating session check that the screws holding the blade on to the boot are adequately tightened and that the edges are free of any rust. If there is rust, make sure you dry your skates properly and store them without their guards. Guards should only be used when carrying skates or for walking on any surface other than ice – **never for storage purposes**.

Your boots must be cleaned on a regular basis with the relevant colour leather restorer, and every couple of months – or more frequently if you skate often – your blades must be sharpened (reground). Your blade manufacturer or local rink will provide this service.

Safety

In order to have a safe and enjoyable time when skating, you must observe a few basic rules. Unless instructed otherwise, skate in one direction only (anti-clockwise) and keep to the outside of the rink. Your speed should be the same or slightly lower than the rink norm. Be considerate towards others and always look where you are going. Keep the centre of the rink clear for those skaters practising or taking professional instruction, and always follow the instructions given by ice rink stewards/supervisors or professional coaches. Wear gloves at all times! Under-fives must always wear head protection (such as a woollen hat or ice hockey helmet). Never take food, drink or cigarettes on to the ice.

The rink

The ice rink or ice *pad*, as it is also known, is a large area specifically designated for ice skating. Most rinks are 56–60 m (61–66 yds) in length and 26–30 m (28–33 yds) in width. The edges are marked by a wooden or plastic barrier (also known as the *boards*) approximately 1 m (1 yd) in height, which can be used to assist the new skater until he gains balance.

On the technical side, ice is made by pumping various freezing chemicals through pipes set in concrete (the rink floor). The ice will be around 5 cm (2 in) in depth, and is resurfaced many times each day using a Zamboni or Polar Bear resurfacer. These amazing machines scrape and cut the ice surface, depositing a layer of warm water at the same time. (A resurface generally takes about 15 minutes.)

The rink will most probably be surrounded by rubber matting (in order to protect the skaters' blades) and banks of seats, arena-style, for spectators to watch the on-ice activities.

First steps

After checking that your boots are correctly fastened and your blades clear of any debris (paper or chewing gum, for example), take hold of the right-hand side of the barrier at the entrance to the ice. (Don't forget to wear your gloves!)

Stage 1

● Stand with your feet together (if necessary holding on to the barrier, or a friend, with your right hand). Hold your arms out to the side at about waist level.
● Turn your feet to form a letter *L*, with the right foot pointing forwards.
● Bend both knees and slide the right foot forwards.
● Lift your left foot and place it down next to the right.
● Form the feet into another letter *L*, with the left foot leading, and repeat.

If this proves too difficult, start out by simply walking on the ice. Even if you do start this way, you will find that after a short time you are gliding along.

▲ *Standing up on the ice*   ▲ *Pushing off*

Gliding ▶

It is very important to keep your arms absolutely still, held out to the side. This will feel unnatural, but if your arms do move they will swing, causing you to turn and ultimately lose your balance.

Stage 2

● Stand in a letter *L* position with your right foot leading (as before, your arms should be held firmly to the side with your hands at about waist height).

● Bend both knees and slide the right foot forwards, stretching your left foot and leg back at the end of the push. (This back leg or *free* leg should be straight, with the foot turned outwards.)

● Hold this position for about two counts (if possible), and then repeat on the other side.

The free leg/foot is the non-skating leg/foot, so that if you are standing on the right foot it is the left, and vice versa. Make sure the skating knee is always bent!

Stage 3

- Stand in your letter *L* position with the right foot leading.
- Following the instructions given for *Stage 2*, try to be aware of the sides of the skate (or *edges*) you are using.
- The pushing foot should be tilted slightly to the *inside* (by pressing on the inside of that foot). The push must be from the blade of the skate – *not* the toe.
- The skating foot should be tilted slightly to the *outside*.
- Make sure that you bend the skating knee and keep the free leg straight, with the free foot turned outwards at right angles to it.
- Hold the position for at least three counts/seconds.

How to get up after a fall

Falling is as much a part of ice skating as any other move. As a result there is a rather over-used saying, 'Falling is a sign of improvement', meaning that if you fall, at least you are becoming a little adventurous and not just trying movements within your capabilities.

10

▲ *Getting up after a fall*

Generally falls do not hurt the skater or cause damage – you just slide and the slide absorbs most of the force. When you want to get back on your feet, turn on to your side and from that position roll on to your hands and knees. Holding yourself steady with your hands, place your stronger foot on the ice in front of you and push upwards. Now stand with your feet together.

The dip

This is an excellent move to practise bending your knees, and at the same time it will help you to gain confidence. Stand with your feet together, and your arms held out firmly to the side. Now bend your knees and touch the underneath of your skates, then return to your standing position. (This is a good movement for small children, who can practise falling over at the same time.)

How to stop

Snowplough

● Skate forwards and gather a little speed.
● Hold your arms out to the side.
● Stand with your feet about 0.5 m (18 in) apart and your knees bent.
● Turn your toes inwards, press on the inside edges and push the feet slightly further apart, keeping the knees bent the whole time and arms absolutely still.

Your skates will skid sideways, your left foot moving to the left, your right foot moving to the right, acting like brakes. Don't let the skates get too far apart or you might end up in a very awkward position.

T stop

Gather some speed, then stand on your stronger foot and turn the back foot out at right angles to the skating foot. Now, without putting much weight on this foot, place it down, tilted to the inside and drag it gently along the ice until you stop.

▲ *The dip*

11

▲ *Snowplough stop*   ▲ *T stop*

How to skate backwards

Stage 1 (or 'backward sculling')

● Check first that there are no skaters in your line of travel.

● Bend both knees and turn your toes inwards to form an inverted letter *V*.
● Pressing on the insides of your feet (your inside edges), push your skates apart. (Both skates should be travelling together at the same speed.)
● Straighten your knees slightly and draw the heels together.
● Repeat.

When you feel comfortable with this move try the next stage.

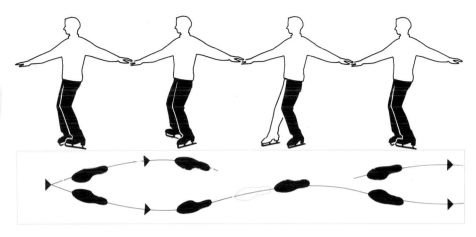

▲ *Fig.1 Pushing backwards*

- Now bring them close together, then lift one foot in front. (Try to hold the foot in front of you for a second or two.)
- Bring the feet back together, repeat the push and lift the other foot in front.

During this movement, make sure that you keep your arms still, with your hands at about (or slightly below) waist height. **Always look where you are going.**

How to stop

Bend both knees and stand with your feet approximately 0.5 m (18 in) apart. Now press on your inside edges and push the skates apart.

Stage 2

- Start with your toes turned inwards.
- Press on your inside edges and push the feet apart so that your skates are moving at the same time and at the same speed.
- When your feet are about 0.5 m (18 in) apart, lift one foot across and place it down at the side of the other.
- Repeat the move, stepping to the other side.

You should now be travelling backwards in a straight line. **Always look where you are going.**

Stage 3

If you can manage *Stage 2* without too many problems, then you are ready to try the next stage.

- Start as before.
- Push the feet apart.

More advanced moves

Your edges

An ice skate has two edges: an outside and an inside. These edges correspond to the outside and inside of your foot. The underside of an ice skate is ground hollow to achieve this result. Most pushing involves using inside edges, and most good forward and backward skating involves standing on outside edges.

Standing on both edges at the same time is known as skating a *flat* and it is a major fault in skating. Bearing this information in mind, the following pages will deal more specifically with the individual edges.

Forward outside edges

Left foot

- Stand with your feet together and knees bent.
- Skating in an anti-clockwise direction

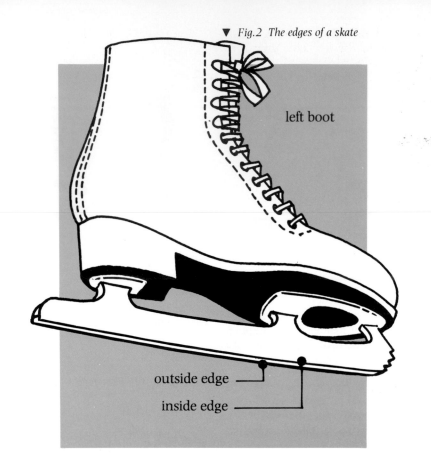

▼ *Fig.2 The edges of a skate*

left boot

outside edge

inside edge

outside edge (1)

side edge (2)

▲ *Forward outside edge (2)*

15

Forward inside edges

Right foot

● Moving in an anticlockwise direction, take three forward pushes, starting with the right foot.
● Glide forwards on to your right foot with your left arm leading.
● Now lean with your whole body to the left, stretching your free leg back as you do so.

Your skate should fall slightly inwards and you will be travelling on an inside edge.

Left foot

Moving in an anti-clockwise direction with the right arm leading, take three pushes, starting with the left foot. Now glide on to the left foot, stretching your free leg back and turning out your free foot.

Forward inside edge (1) ▶

▲ *Forward in*

16

Backward outside edges

Right foot

This is a far more tricky movement than you might think!

- Skating in an anti-clockwise direction with the right arm held back and the left arm leading, glide backwards on to the right foot.
- Lift the free foot (the left) and hold it so that it is directly in front of the skating foot (the right).
- As your skate touches the ice, stretch up the free side of your body (the left), so that you are leaning towards the outside edge.
- Hold the position for three seconds, or as long as possible.

Sometimes it's easier if you take three or five pushes instead of just one.

Left foot

For the left foot, move in a clockwise direction and reverse the above instructions, substituting right for left and left for right. (Watch out for any fellow skaters who might be in your line of travel!)

◀ *Backward outside edge*

Forward crossovers

The usual way of getting round corners involves a move called a *crossover*.

Anti-clockwise

● Leading with the right arm, glide forwards on to an outside edge on the left foot (keeping your left knee bent all the time).

● Now lift your right foot and cross it over the left, placing it down on to an inside edge.
● Lift the back foot (the left) and place it down at the side of the right foot.
● Repeat the movement.

If you skate consecutive crossovers you will complete a circle.

Clockwise

Crossovers can also be skated in the other direction, starting on the right foot with the left arm leading. The same instructions apply, substituting right for left and left for right.

▲ *Forward crossover (1)*

◄ *Forward crossover (2)*

Backward crossovers

Anti-clockwise

- Skate backwards in an anti-clockwise direction, holding your left arm in front and your right arm behind.
- Glide backwards on to an outside edge on the right foot. Lift the left foot and cross it over the right.
- Place it down on an inside edge.
- Draw the right foot back.
- Repeat the movement.

Always look where you are going.

Clockwise

For the other side (*clockwise*), reverse the instructions, substituting right for left and left for right.

▲ *Backward crossover (1)*   ▲ *Backward crossover (2)*

Stepping from backwards to forwards

This move involves skating backwards on one foot, turning 180° and stepping forwards on to the other.

● Start with the right foot. Place your feet together, with your arms held out to the side. (Your knees must be slightly bent.)

● Glide backwards on to your right foot, lifting your free foot (the left) in front as you do so.

● Bring your feet together and glide on to your left foot and finally on to your right.

● Standing with the left foot in front, take your left shoulder back and turn your head in the same direction.

● Place your heels together and step forwards on to an outside edge on the left foot, drawing back the right shoulder as you do so.

● Hold the forward outside edge.

● If you are starting on the left foot, follow the above instructions, substituting left for right and right for left. You must also turn in the other direction!

Three turns

This is one of the most frequently used turns in ice skating, and even more so in ice dancing. It involves turning from forwards to backwards (or vice versa), changing edge and direction but not the skating foot.

Left forward outside

● Standing on a bent knee, glide on to the left foot on an outside edge. (You should be gliding in an anti-clockwise direction.)

● Bring the feet close together, and the right arm forwards. Rotate the left hip, waist and upper body.

● Straighten the left knee slightly and (with a little practice) you should end up

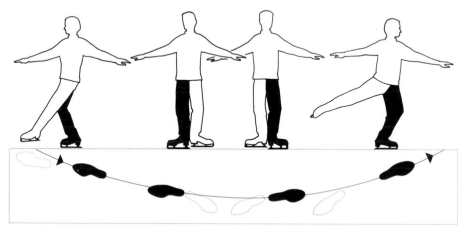

◀ *Fig. 3 Stepping from backwards to forwards*

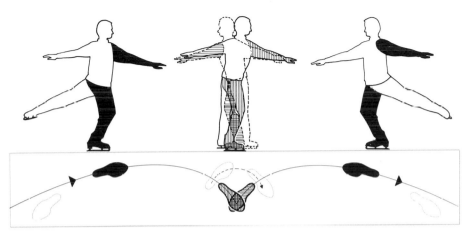

A 'Mohawk' is a very important, effective but reasonably easy skating turn. Mohawks appear all over the place in free skating, ice dancing and ice hockey. The turn involves making a half-turn from either forwards to backwards or backwards to forwards by way of changing feet. The edge going into the turn is the same as the edge coming out, although there is a change of direction. Probably the simplest Mohawks are the *forward insides* which are explained here.

skating backwards on the same foot on an inside edge, having completed a 180° turn.

Make sure the turn is completed on one foot only.

Right forward outside

- With the right arm leading, glide in a clockwise direction on to an outside edge.
- Now bring the feet together, with the left shoulder in front. Rotate the right hip, waist and upper body.

▲ *Fig.4 Three turns*

- Straighten the skating knee slightly, and you should be sliding backwards on the same foot, having completed the turn.

When three turns are included in ice dances, they generally involve an additional push and change of feet. After the turn has been completed, the skater pushes on to a backward outside edge on the other foot, holding the free foot in front for several seconds.

Right forward inside

- Facing in an anti-clockwise direction, with the right foot and left arm leading, glide on to an inside edge.
- Bring the heel of the left foot to the middle (instep) of the right foot.
- Move the right arm and shoulder forwards.
- Keeping the free foot turned out as much as possible, change feet so that you are travelling backwards on an inside edge on the left foot. **Always look in the direction of travel!**

Left forward inside

● Facing clockwise, with the left foot and right arm leading, glide on to an inside edge.
● Bring the heel of the right foot to the instep of the left foot, and the left shoulder in front.
● Change the arms and skating foot so that you are travelling backwards on the inside edge on the right foot.

Free skating

Free skating involves jumps, spins, various artistic movements and steps put to music. It is usually performed individually, but is also part of pair skating (*see* page 26).

If you are interested in free skating, then you will need to buy the right equipment. Strong boots and specifically designed blades with a good series of toe picks (the serrated points at the front of each skate) are essential for the more advanced movements of the type seen on television. Although there

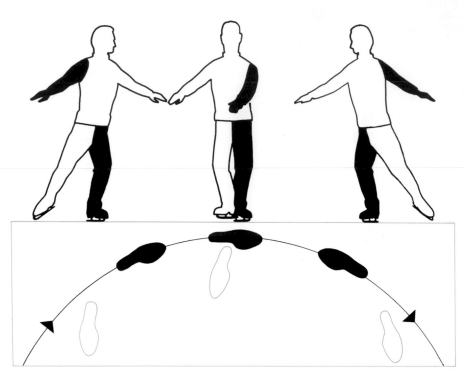

▲ *Fig.5 Left-foot Mohawk*

are a few movements you can try without lessons, any others not covered by this book should be taught by a good skater or professional coach.

Jumping on ice

Few things in life can match the thrill of moving fast across the ice, jumping, turning in the air and landing perfectly without any apparent loss of speed. Most jumps on ice, involve taking off and landing backwards (almost always on outside edges). Skating jumps also involve rotating in the air (either clockwise or anti-clockwise according to preference), and taking off and landing on one foot only. Single jumps have one turn, doubles have two and triples three. (The exceptions are the *axel* jumps which involve one-and-a-half turns for a single, two-and-a-half for a double and three-and-a-half for a triple.)

Three jump or waltz jump

This movement involves jumping from a forward outside edge (left or right foot), making a half turn in the air, and landing backwards on the other foot with the free leg stretched back.

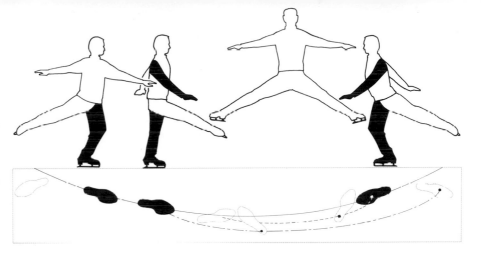

▲ *Fig.6 Three jump or waltz jump*

Spins

Spins form an important and very beautiful part of free skating. It is usual to spin in one direction (either clockwise or anti-clockwise and usually rotating in the same direction chosen for the jumps) and on one foot only. There are quite a few spins involving different positions, combinations of positions and jumps into and from spinning positions.

23

Basic spin

Before you attempt a spin you should try to determine your natural spinning direction.

● Stand with your feet slightly apart and knees bent.
● Take your right shoulder back.
● Now push a little with your right foot at the same time as bringing the right shoulder strongly forwards. You should start to turn to the left.

Try the same movements, starting with your left shoulder back and pushing with the left foot. Whichever direction feels the easiest is most likely your natural spinning direction. (For most people this is anti-clockwise.)

Standing spin

● Stand with your feet slightly apart and your arms held out at waist height.
● Place your right toe in the ice.
● Take your right shoulder back.
● Push with your toe and bring your right shoulder forward, lifting your right foot off the ice at the end of the push and placing it against your lower left leg with the toe pointing downwards.

▲ *Spiral*

● Bring your arms together.
● When you want to stop, open out your arms and place your right toe back in the ice.

For those of you who prefer the other spinning direction, reverse these instructions, substituting left for right and right for left.

Spiral

This involves gathering speed, pushing on to (for example) the left foot, leaning forward and raising the free leg until it is in line with your head. The arms should be held out to the side. The head is held up, and both the skating and the free leg should be straight. The free foot (the non-standing foot) should be turned out at right angles to the skating foot. Before skating, get the feel of this position by holding the barrier with one hand and raising your leg.

24

Compulsory figures

Compulsory figures are the various circles and eights incorporating all important skating edges, directions and turns. Until recently they formed a major part of all free-skating championships. Due to objections from the media that they were boring to watch, they were dropped from international competition, but the NISA still has skating tests consisting of these figures.

The most basic figure is called a *forward outside eight* and is performed in the following way.

- Stand with your feet together.
- Bend both knees and form your feet into a letter L with your right foot and arm leading.
- Push on to the right foot and stretch the free foot back, raising the free side of your body as you do so.
- Bring your feet together, leaving the free foot raised.

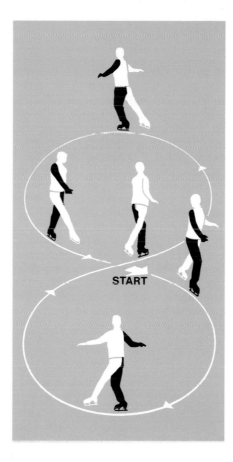

- After you have travelled more than half-way around the circle, bring the free foot in front and change the leading arm.
- When you have returned to your starting point or *centre*, bring the feet together, forming another letter L with your feet.
- Place your left arm in front and push on to the left foot.
- When you are more than half-way around the circle, change the arm and bring the free foot in front...

Figures are skated either three or four times, depending upon which of the several dozen you are practising. It should be said that your tracings must be very accurate representations of circles and consist of strong edges. Each subsequent tracing should be placed as close as possible to its predecessor.

◀ *Fig.7 Forward outside eight*

◄ Pair skating

Pair skating

Pair skating is probably the most exciting, intricate and spectacular skating discipline. All the elements of ice dancing, free skating and compulsory figures are combined and integrated at great speed, with the addition of overhead lifts, throws and pair spins. For decades the Russian skaters have dominated this field, with a few notable exceptions from North America.

Anyone wishing to pair skate should try to find a partner of similar standard, age and physique. Ideally the boy/man should be very strong – in fact most top pair skaters train with weights – and both parties must be first-class free skaters. Good professional instruction is recommended.

Ice dancing

This area of skating is one of the most popular with both recreational and top-level competitors.

Equipment

The equipment used by ice dancers is slightly different from that used in other disciplines. The boots are generally softer and more flexible. The blades are markedly different, being both shorter at the back and often thinner (the distance between the two edges being less than with free skating blades). It is by no means essential for ice dancers to wear specifically designed dance blades.

There are several competition sections in ice dancing, the first and probably most popular amongst older skaters being known as the 'compulsory dances'.

Compulsory dances

These amount to various set steps performed with a partner to a set rhythm. Compulsory dances are largely based on ballroom dancing. In competition all skaters must perform exactly the same steps and place each move on the same designated areas of the ice surface. It is usual to skate either two or three sequences of each dance. Those dances with patterns that do not involve a complete circuit of the rink are usually skated four times, while those that do involve the full circuit are skated twice.

Original dance

This section forms part of the major championships. It consists of an original routine devised by each competing couple, who interpret whatever tempo and character (quickstep, tango, waltz) has been set down in the rules for that competition. The routine has a duration of two minutes (within a ten-second margin), and the couple are free to move around the ice in either direction with many restrictions, which change from year to year with the rhythms chosen. Usually only two pieces of music are allowed; and skaters must not include lifts in their routine.

Ice dancing: free dance ▶

◀ *Open hold*

Open hold

This hold is used to start and gather speed. Both partners skate forwards, each holding the other by only one hand. The joining arm is held out almost straight, with the girl usually slightly in front of the boy. This hold is generally used as the starting position for compulsory dances.

Kilian hold

● Both partners face the same direction, with the girl on the right-hand side of the boy.

● The boy's right hand rests on the girl's right hip bone, and is held in place by her right hand.

● The girl's left arm is straight and held across the boy's upper body.

● The boy holds the girl's left hand with his left hand.

● The couple should be standing as close together as possible.

For the canasta tango, the couple change sides (reverse Kilian), and the boy takes the place of the girl.

Free dance

This a routine lasting up to four mintues (three minutes for junior and four minutes for senior events) which enables the skaters to show off their technical and artistic skills relating to footwork, small low lifts, general originality and ability to interpret their music.

The skaters are allowed to use various pieces of music of different tempo and character, with no restriction placed on the theme they choose to interpret.

The holds

There are various holds used in ice dancing. Here are some of the most popular.

Variation of a waltz hold ◀

Kilian hold ▶

Basic ice dance steps

Forward *chassé*

● Glide on to an outside edge on your left foot.
● Bring your feet together, change feet and raise the left foot a couple of inches above the ice, so that you are standing on an inside edge on the right foot.
● Bring the feet back together and glide on to the other outside edge, on the left foot.

The right foot *chassé* is completed in the same way but starting on the right. The length of time allowed for each step is dependent upon what dance is being skated.

▼ *Fig.8 Forward* chassé

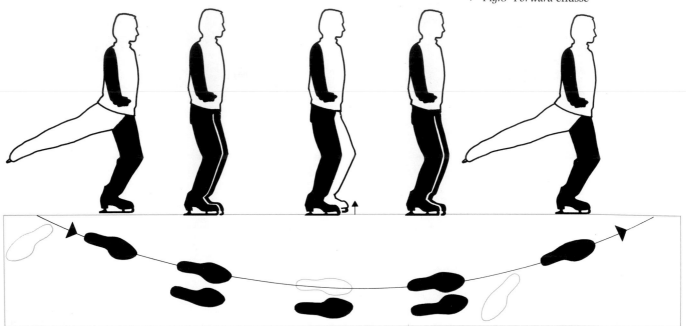

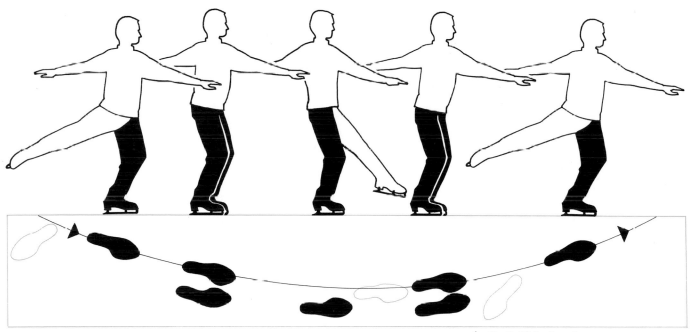

▲ Fig. 9 *Slide* chassé

Slide *chassé*

● Skate on to an outside edge on the left foot, stretching your free leg back.

● Bring your feet together, change feet and slide the left foot in front. (You will now be standing on an inside edge on the right foot.)

● Bring the feet back together.

For the right foot, follow the instructions given above, but start on the right.

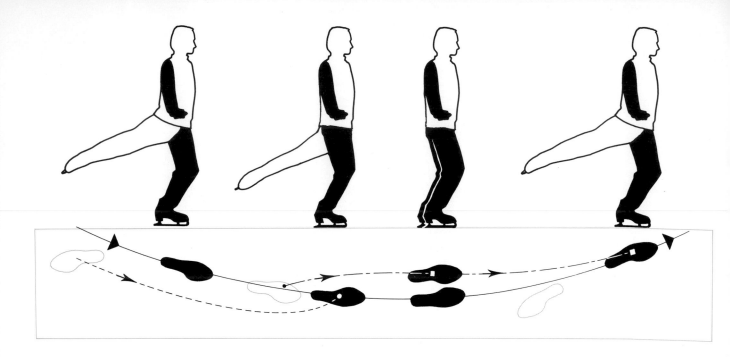

Forward run or progressive

The forward run involves a series of steps running either clockwise or anti-clockwise.

● Skate the first step on to an outside edge, and the second on to an inside edge.

● On the second step, place the free foot down on an inside edge, slightly in front and to the side of the skating foot.

● At the same time as this foot touches the ice, stretch the other foot back.

● Now skate another forward outside edge. Each step involves a push.

▲ *Fig.10 Forward run or progressive*

Swing roll

This move frequently appears in ice dancing, as it is effective and easy to perform.

- Stand with your feet together and bend both knees.
- Strike on to an outside edge on either foot, stretching the free leg back as you do so.
- Slowly straighten your skating knee at the same time as bringing the free leg in front.
- To finish, bring the feet back together and push on to the other foot.

Cross roll and swing

This move involves standing on an outside edge and then crossing the free foot over and placing it down on an outside edge. This is followed by a swing roll of the free foot.

It is generally skated on the left foot, crossing the right foot over, followed by a right foot (outside edge) swing, bringing the left foot in front.

Dutch waltz

This dance can be skated either with or without a partner. The hold used must be the Kilian (*see* page 28), with the girl standing on the right side of the boy. Forward skating is all that is required and both parties skate the same steps, hopefully at the same time.

- Opening steps: start by pushing on to an outside edge on your left foot, followed by a cross on to an inside edge on the right foot.
- The dance starts with a run/progressive (*see* page 32) to the left, an outside left edge and two swing rolls, firstly to the right, then to the left.
- Run/progressive to the right, outside right edge, and bring the feet together.
- Now push on to an outside on the left foot, followed by an inside on the right foot.
- Finish with a run/progressive to the left, an outside left edge, followed by a swing roll to the right.
- Repeat the sequence.

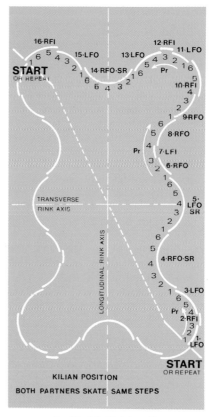

▲ *Fig.11 Dutch waltz*

Canasta tango

The hold is reverse Kilian (the girl stands on the left of the boy), and both parties skate the same steps.

● Push on to a left forward outside edge, followed by a right forward outside, and then a forward run/progressive to the left.

● Follow this with a left foot forward *chassé*, followed by a swing roll on the left foot.

● The feet are brought back together, followed by a slide *chassé* on the right foot.

● Next, skate a swing roll on the right foot, followed by a slide *chassé* on the left foot, followed by a left foot run/progressive, an outside left edge and a cross roll on to the right foot.

● Repeat the steps, starting from the forward run/progressive to the left.

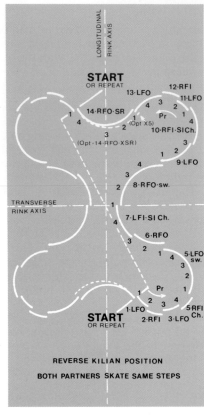

▲ *Fig.12 Canasta tango*

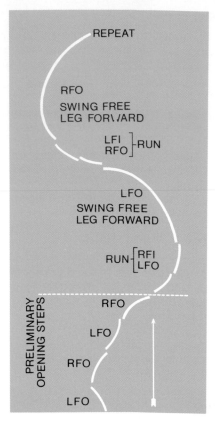

▲ *Fig.13 Preliminary foxtrot*

34

Preliminary foxtrot

This dance is skated in Kilian hold. There are usually four introductory steps (left, right, left, right, all on outside edges), followed by a forward run/ progressive (two steps) and an outside swing roll. This is followed by exactly the same sequence, but starting on the other foot and skating in the other direction.

Dance intervals

Most ice rinks *dance intervals* which generally consist of a 15-minute period (often during the public sessions), specifically allocated for the ice dancers to skate their steps to the correct music.

The ice is cleared of all non-dancers and approximately ten dances are skated consecutively to music of the relevant tempo. During these dance intervals you will be able to skate with your partner (if you have one), other dancers, or your professional coach.

It is well worth attending some dance intervals at your local rink; better still, employ a good professional coach to teach you how to perform the steps and sequences correctly.

Dance clubs

You can also practise ice dancing during your local dance club session. Dance clubs are an excellent way of helping you to improve your skating standard in company with other members. Clubs usually rent an hour or more of ice time each week from the rink, during which they play their own choice of dance music.

Dance clubs often provide for group or individual tuition by the rink professional coaches, as well as organising small monthly competitions for their members. They are good places to meet new partners – skating or otherwise. (Dance clubs may insist on a certain minimum standard in order to belong, but your local rink will be able to advise you on this.)

Precision skating

In 1990 a new discipline – precision skating – was introduced to the sport both nationally and internationally. Precision skating involves skaters in various group formations performing steps to music. This type of skating, which originated in Canada, is one of the fastest-growing areas of the sport, and one in which most skaters can take part. Many rinks now have precision teams, with armies of fundraisers working together to find the money for various overseas trips to competitions.

Precision skating has proved very popular with skaters of all ages who wish to compete as a team rather than individually. The most important distinguishing features of precision skating are the accuracy of the skating and the various moves performed (block moves), and the way in which the team skates as one entity.

The groups or 'teams' may consist of girls, boys, or a combination of both, with a maximum of six alternates allowed. There are specific categories

▲ *Precision skaters*

based on age groups into which teams must fit. Any team from a particular category will skate against other teams of the same category. At the moment there are five categories, of which only junior and senior teams skate internationally.

- **Juvenile** team of between 12 and 20 members. Skaters must be under the age of 12 on the 1st January preceding the event. The programme length is four minutes.
- **Novice** team of between 12 and 20 members under the age of 14 on the 1st January preceding the event. Programme length is three-and-a-half minutes.
- **Junior** team of between 12 and 20 skaters, each of whom must be at least 12 but not 19 on 1 July preceding the competition. Programme length is four minutes.
- **Senior** team of between 21 and 24 skaters – each must be at least 12 years old (no upper age limit). Programme length is four-and-a-half minutes.
- **Adult** team of between 12 and 24 skaters. They must be aged over 20 years on the 1st January preceding the event, and 75% of the team must be

over the age of 25. Programme length is three-and-a-half minutes.

Music

The music used must be appropriate for the skaters. It has to consist of three distinct rhythms of at least two different tempos. Vocals can be included in professional – but not in amateur – competitions.

The costumes must also be appropriate, taking into account the age and appearance of the skaters, and reflecting the character of the music.

Competition and test skating

Competition skating

There are various kinds of competitions available for skaters of all standards and in each of the disciplines. The most basic competitions take place within the skating clubs attached to rinks. (Virtually all rinks have skating clubs, and most have a notice board with relevant information for both club and non-club members.) These minor competitions provide the perfect opportunity for new up-and-coming skaters to make their debut. For the free skaters this may involve skating a simple programme of a minute or so duration, including just a few basic jumps, spins, spirals and steps.

A competition probably provides the first opportunity for a small child to skate by himself in front of an audience, and can do wonders for his self-esteem. Competitions also allow skating peers to compare themselves and their progress in a pleasant, friendly atmosphere.

There are various 'open competitions' available to skaters. 'Open' generally means open to skaters of the appropriate standard and age group (or whatever the organisers stipulate). The competitions are held under the regulations of, and in accordance with, a permit granted by the Ice Figure Committee.

Test skating

The skating organisations in all the major skating countries have devised a series of proficiency tests to assess the appropriate achievement level of skaters in all disciplines. In the UK, the tests run from either 'Novice' or 'Preliminary' (depending upon the discipline) through to 'Gold'. Gold medal skaters are really top competitors, so the standard of their skating is very high indeed. Top-level skaters sometimes go on to teach or judge.

Participation in most competitons or championships is dependent upon having achieved a predetermined test level. (For further information on this, contact the National Ice Skating Association.)

Championships

In all skating countries there are various championships open to up-and-coming skaters. In order to compete you must have passed the relevant skating proficiency tests, and in some cases it is necessary to have been selected. There are usually age restrictions for novice and junior events but not for senior events. In national events it is usual to be a resident of the relevant country. (There are occasionally exceptions to this rule, which allow a person born in one country to compete for another.)

International events

There are various international events open by invitation to top competitors, and most of the major skating countries hold such events. There are also the Novice, Junior and Senior National Championships, followed by the European (non-European skaters are excluded), World and Olympic events.

Judging

The judging of ice skating events is less complicated than it may appear. The following pages explain the major points that the judges look for in each discipline. There is always an odd number of judges on a skating panel, usually five, seven or nine, plus a referee to supervise. All marks are taken out of a maximum score of six.

Ice dancing

Compulsory dance

The skaters must dance in time to the music, and the couple must skate in unison (as one). Strong edges must be apparent, together with good use of the ice surface, and the designated pattern across the ice must be adhered to at all times. There is one mark from each judge.

Original dance

The judges look for originality, difficulty, interpretation, strong edges and good use of ice. There are two sets of marks from each judge: one for composition and one for presentation.

Free dance

The skaters are marked on the basis of their speed, unison and use of the ice, together with their style and interpretative capabilities. There are two marks awarded: one for technical merit, one for artistic impression.

Free skating

The criteria the judges look for include the quality of skating edges, style and soft movement over the ice, together with carriage, flow and utilisation of the available space. There is no pre-set mark; instead, at the end of the performances jumps, spins, steps, etc. are compared with those of previous skaters, and marks are then determined.

Original free or technical programme

This programme is a routine devised by or for each skater in the championship, and must last less than two minutes and 40 seconds. It will contain certain pre-selected moves that all the skaters must complete, including certain jumps and jump combinations, spins and jump spins. (The combination jump occurs when the landing edge of the first jump becomes the take-off edge for the second, without touching down with the free foot, unless the end jump is a 'toe' jump.) A more difficult second jump will earn higher marks than a simpler one, but apparent ease of execution is an important factor. There are two marks: one for technical merit, one for artistic impression.

Long free programme

In international competitions this is now four-and-a-half minutes for men and four minutes for women. There are no set elements, but the skaters take the opportunity to show the judges their greatest skills. The judges are looking for high technical content, sureness and style. Jumps that are repeated can only be given an additional mark if they form part of a combination. There are two marks: one for technical merit and one for artistic impression.

Pair skating

Original technical programme

This programme should contain various specified lifts and pair spins, together with solo jumps, spins and step sequences. There are no throws in the technical programme. Two marks are awarded by each judge: one for technical merit and one for artistic impression.

Long programme

The most important factor here is unison, together with speed, grace, strong edges and best use of the available ice surface. Technical content, in the form of difficult lifts, throws and pair spins, together with free skating solo jumps and spins, is very important. There are two marks from each judge: one for technical merit and one for artistic impression.

Precision skating

The skaters are marked first for the composition of their routine, and then for their presentation. The composition refers to such aspects as originality, technical difficulty, placement of the various manoeuvres on the ice, cleanness and sureness, continuous skating on edges with speed and flow, and smooth and precise transitions. Presentation covers unison, musical synchronisation, carriage and style. The variety of music and movements in time with the music must reflect both the ages and abilities of the skaters. The harmonious composition of the programme and its conformity to the music must also be taken into consideration.

Final places

The important thing to note when trying to work out the final position of skaters in a particular event is the fact that it is the skater with the *lowest number of place marks*, not the one with the highest marks, that wins. The place marks are based on the individual positions in which skaters are placed by each judge. The total number of place marks given by each judge to each skater is calculated, then compared, and the final result is reached. For example, should one judge place a skater first, another place that skater second, and a

third place that skater third, then the total number of the judges' places equals six. Any skater who has a higher total of place marks will be positioned lower, and any skater with less marks will be placed higher than that skater. The winner will have the least number of place marks, while the skater placed last will have the highest number.

Stroking

Stroking is the umbrella term used for all good forward and backward skating, control of edges, and the ability to turn well in all directions and to skate accurately in time to music.

In North America, where I started my life as a professional coach, we would start most free skating sessions with 15 minutes of practice stroking. Within a few sessions we would choreograph a 15-minute routine, incorporating as many relevant moves as possible, to music the skaters liked (usually records from the top end of the charts). The skaters would learn this routine after a

couple of sessions and from then on would skate the routine in much the same way as the precision skaters (without the block moves), as a very effective warm-up exercise.

Ice hockey

Ice hockey is one of the most popular sports in the world. The game was probably exported from the north of England by British soldiers who used to play a form of it during the long winters. It has been a recognised sport since the end of the last century, and the great prize is the Stanley Cup (first played for in 1894), donated by Lord Stanley, the Governor-General of Canada at that time.

Equipment

Two teams of six skaters play using wooden sticks which are limited in length to 147 cm (58 in), with a 32 cm (12 in) blade. The goalminder is permitted a slightly heavier and wider blade. The 'puck' is made of vulcanised rubber, 7.62 cm (3 in) in diameter, 2.52 cm (1 in) in width and weighing 156–170 g (5.5–6 oz).

The players wear heavy protective clothing, including a helmet, knee and elbow pads, and shoulder and shin guards. They also wear thick gloves and long socks topped off by shorts and sweaters in the relevant team colours. The goalminders wear additional protection, including leg guards, chest protectors, face masks and extra padded gloves.

The boots are quite different from figure boots, with lower internal supports and protective toe and heel caps, moulded arch supports and tendon-protectors. The blades are narrow and reinforced by hollow tubing.

The rink

Olympic size rinks, 60 × 30 m (65 × 33 yds), are ideal for ice hockey, although it can be played on smaller surfaces. It is usual to have a plexi-glass screen or netting placed on top of the barriers/boards; to protect the spectators from the puck and to keep it in play.

The surface is marked up as follows: red goal lines are drawn approximately 3 m (10 ft) from each end of the rink on which the goals, 1.22 m (4 ft) in height and 1.88 m (6 ft) in width, are placed. For safety reasons the goals are not fixed to the ice. The goals have a net at the back to hold the puck. Two blue lines divide the ice surface into three zones: defence, neutral and attacking. Defence refers to the zone nearest one's own goal; neutral is the central area of the rink; while the attacking zone is that nearest the opponent's goal.

There is a red line running across the centre of the rink between the two blue lines. A blue spot inside a large red circle marks the centre of the rink. There are also four red circles, two in each half, which are known as the face-off spots. Alongside each of these, red lines 60 cm (23 in) long run parallel to the goal lines. There are additional red lines, 90 cm (35 in) in length, which run from the outer edge of all four red circles. In the centre zone there are two red spots, placed at a distance of 1.5 m (5 ft) from each blue line, midway between the side barriers.

The game

The game lasts for 60 minutes, split into three periods of 20 minutes. The time is counted only when the puck is in play. Although only six players are allowed on the ice at any one time, there are no restrictions on the number of substitutions each team can make.

There are two referees for amateur matches (one for each half of the ice). For National Hockey League (NHL) matches there is just one referee, together with two linesmen. Their major function is to signal with a whistle when offsides occur.

The face-off

The game begins with the 'face-off', when the referee drops the puck on to the ice in the centre of the rink, between the sticks of the 'centremen' of each team. (A face-off also occurs when there has been some form of misplay.) Under such circumstances the face-off will be taken at the nearest marked point on the ice surface.

The puck only becomes dead in two circumstances: first if it is hit over the barrier/boards; and second in the event of some violation of the rules. The puck must enter the attacking zone ahead of the player.

A goal can only be scored using a stick, and will be discounted if there is an opposing player in the relevant goal crease. In the event of a goal being scored, a goal judge will switch on a red light in the relevant goal.

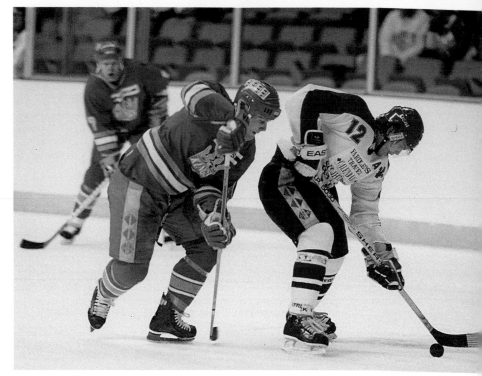

Rough play is penalised by way of the 'penalty box', into which players can be sent for two minutes or more in the event of certain rule infringements.

▲ *Ice hockey*

Speed skating

Speed skaters are the fastest-moving self-propelled sports people over level ground. There are two types of speed skating: *long track* and *short track*. Long track uses very large, purpose-built speed tracks. Skaters compete against a

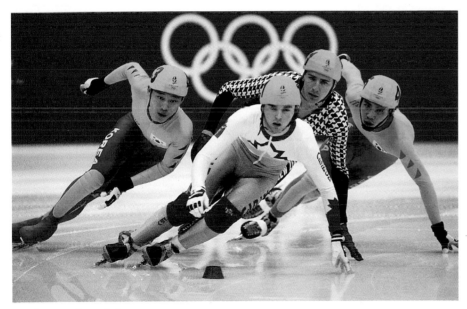

▲ *Short-track speed skating*

▲ *Long-track speed skating*

clock and their various times are then compared to achieve the overall results. Short track, which involves racing against other skaters, can be skated on most Olympic-size ice rinks.

Equipment

Speed boots have much lower internal supports than either hockey or figure boots, and the blades are much longer and flatter. In short track, the boots are generally made of a combination of fibre glass and leather. The blades are shorter than those used in long track, in order to ensure maximum grip when cornering on small rinks.

Speed skaters wear close-fitting lycra suits. All short-track skaters are obliged to wear protective hard-shell helmets and gloves, but these are optional for long-track skaters. Safety pads are placed against the barriers to protect skaters in the event of a collision.

There are various race distances and categories of competitor according to age. (More information can be obtained from the National Ice Skating Association.)

Group skating lesson ▶

Ice skating careers

Teaching

Many of the top skaters, whether they are high-standard test medallists or competitors, end their careers as professional coaches employed by a rink or group of rinks on a freelance basis. Coaches either pay some kind of agreed rent to the rink or a percentage of their lesson fee. If you have at least a silver medal, can relate well to people and are prepared to work the anti-social hours (your working hours are generally other people's leisure hours), you might enjoy coaching.

Nearly all skating lessons last for 15 minutes and take place on an individual basis. (It must be said, however, that both newcomers and advanced skaters can be trained very effectively in groups.)

Ice shows

'Holiday On Ice' is probably the best-known ice show, designed to appeal to all age groups and people from all walks of life. There are various companies touring around the world, playing to packed houses, using the biggest skating names for the lead roles, in order to thrill and entertain. The chorus consists of less well known but still very accomplished skaters.

There is a constant demand for both lead and chorus skaters, but there are various minimum requirements with regard to age, appearance and skating standard. (Basically, you have to be a good skater and look very nice!)

Management

As a result of the huge growth in ice rink construction in recent years, there is a continuing demand for suitably qualified people to organise, run and promote them. Gone are the days when this type of work could be learned on site, and a suitable university or college qualification is now a must. In addition, you must be a good skater. As long as you are personable, well organised and able to lead a harmonious team, then this field could be for you.

Judging

Skating judges are usually former top-level skaters. They will have decided to forgo income from the sport in order to give their time, free of charge, to judge skating tests and competitions at levels corresponding to their own skating standard. (For more information on this, contact the National Ice Skating Association.)

Ice skating fitness/preparation

Although ice skating will make your body stronger, it is still a good idea to take some additional exercise to get into shape. Obviously, the parts of the body that are going to take the strain are the legs and feet. However, you should work for good overall fitness to meet the stamina demands of skating fast around an ice rink for hours each week.

You can achieve this standard of fitness in several ways. For instance, you could sign up for exercise classes at your local fitness centre, and perhaps ask an instructor to design a specific programme of weight training to develop those muscles which are particularly relevant to ice skating. For young people, especially girls, great care must be taken to ensure the weights are not too heavy. The danger is that their thigh muscles become over-developed.

There are also a number of things that you can do without expert help. For example, cycling is first-class exercise for skating since it involves a pushing movement which develops many of the muscles used in ice skating. You can also attend dance classes, which will help to improve both fitness and artistic development. Try to keep as close as possible to your recommended weight/height ratio. Your physical shape is very important in ice skating competitions, and the more aesthetically pleasing your shape, the more attractive your skating will look.

A recent innovation which has proved to be an excellent off-ice training device is the 'in-line' skate, or *Rollerblade*, now used by many top ice skaters to keep their muscles in shape. This is particularly so in Canada, where many figure and hockey skaters use their in-liners to keep their feet in the sport when their ice rinks are closed for

the summer. These skates replicate almost perfectly the feeling of ice skating, and are also a tremendous boon to those skaters who do not have a rink quite so easily to hand, as the techniques are pretty much the same.

▲ *'Holiday on Ice'*

Glossary

Backward outside edge Move involving skating backwards on the outside of the skate

Barrier/boards The plastic wall which marks the edge of the ice

Canasta tango (*see* page 34)

Chassé (*see* page 30)

Compulsory dance Set sequence of steps interpreting a particular character of dance

Compulsory figures Circles skated as figures-of-eight incorporating forward and backward edges and turns of varying degrees of difficulty

Crossover Crossing one foot over the other to effect a gradual turning movement – can be skated backwards or forwards

Dip When the skater bends both knees and touches the underneath of the boots

Double tracking When both skates are on the ice for longer than is necessary to make the push

Drag When the skater bends the skating knee low, stretching the free leg behind and dragging it along the ice

Dutch waltz Compulsory dance

Edge The cutting edge of the skate

Flat When both edges are on the ice at the same time

Free dance Skating programme devised by a dance couple, performed in order to interpret several different musical tempos and lasting for a set period of time

Free leg/foot The non-skating leg/foot

Forward glide When the skater is moving forwards on one foot

Ice rink/ice pad The skating area

Inside edge Edge corresponding to the inside of the foot

Kilian Hold Hold in compulsory dancing

Long free skating programme Programme of fixed length with no pre-specified moves

Mohawk 180° turn from either forwards or backwards, by way of changing feet

NISA National Ice Skating Association of Great Britain

Original dance (*see* ice dancing, page 26)

Outside edge Edge of skate corresponding to the outside of the foot

Pair skating (*see* page 26)

Patch Area of ice reserved specifically for compulsory figure practice

Pattern Design made on the ice surface by a dance or any other movements in free or pair skating

Preliminary foxtrot (*see* dance, page 35)

Progressive (run) Series of consecutive outside and inside edges

Scribe Device used for measuring and checking compulsory figures

Skating foot/leg The foot/leg on which the skater is standing

Skate guards Plastic or rubber blade protectors

Snow plough Method of stopping

Spiral (arabesque) Position performed on either edge, backwards or forwards, where the body is held horizontal and the head is in line with the free foot

Stroke A step on to an edge which involves an increase of speed

Stroking Usual method of skating forwards

Three-waltz jump A jump from a forward outside edge, turning 180° and landing backwards on an outside edge on the other foot

Three turn 180° turn from either forwards or backwards, changing edge but without changing foot

Toe picks The sharp serrated area at the front of the skate

Toe pushing Pushing (incorrectly) by using the picks

Tracing The mark left on the ice by the skate

Trailing When the free foot drags along the ice (when it should in fact be raised)

T stop A method of stopping

Index